DETAIL: SCHOOL OF ATHENS
THE VATICAN, ROME

COVER: RAPHAEL REGARDED MEN OF ARTS, LETTERS AND SCIENCE, MATHEMATICIANS AND PHILOSOPHERS AS HIS TEACHERS. THEIR WORKS WERE HIS MODELS AND INSPIRATION.

IN THIS DETAIL FROM HIS MURAL,

"THE SCHOOL OF ATHENS",

HE HAS PAINTED THE GREEK PHILOSOPHER AND MATHEMATICIAN PYTHAGORAS. A YOUNG STUDENT HOLDS A SLATE WHILE THE MASTER MAKES A PERMANENT ENTRY IN HIS BOOK.

DETAIL, THE FIRE IN THE BORGO   THE VATICAN, ROME

COMPLETE MURAL: THE FIRE IN THE BORGO

DEDICATED TO ADELINE PETER WHOSE RESEARCH
ASSISTANCE NEARED COLLABORATION
ON THE VOLUMES DEVOTED TO RAPHAEL,
MICHELANGELO AND DA VINCI.

WORLD RIGHTS RESERVED BY ERNEST RABOFF AND GEMINI SMITH, INC.

LIBRARY OF CONGRESS CATALOGUE CARD NO. 75-139056   PRINTED IN JAPAN BY TOPPAN

RAPHAEL
SANZIO

By Ernest Raboff

ART
FOR
CHILDREN

A GEMINI SMITH BOOK

EDITED BY BRADLEY SMITH

PUBLISHED BY

DOUBLEDAY & CO., INC.

GARDEN CITY, NEW YORK

RAPHAEL SANZIO WAS BORN ON

APRIL 6, 1483, IN URBINO, ITALY. HE RECEIVED HIS EARLY TRAINING FROM HIS TALENTED FATHER, WHO DIED WHEN RAPHAEL WAS ONLY 11. HIS MOTHER HAD DIED WHEN HE WAS 8 AND THE YOUNG ORPHAN WAS LEFT IN THE CARE OF HIS STEPMOTHER.

BUT SOON, PROBABLY BEFORE HE WAS 16, HE BECAME AN APPRENTICE TO THE FAMOUS ARTIST, PIETRO PERUGINO. BETWEEN THE AGES OF 17 AND 20 HE PAINTED SOME OF HIS FINEST EARLY WORKS.

WHEN BARELY 21, THE YOUNG ARTIST MOVED TO FLORENCE, THE ART CAPITAL OF EUROPE AT THAT TIME. THERE RAPHAEL MET WITH AND STUDIED THE WORKS OF LEONARDO DA VINCI, MICHELANGELO AND OTHER MASTERS OF THE ARTS OF PAINTING AND SCULPTURE.

DRAWING OF RAPHAEL BY RABOFF

BY THE TIME RAPHAEL WAS 26, HE WAS RECOGNIZED AS ONE OF ITALY'S MOST IMPORTANT CREATIVE ARTISTS. HE BECAME POPULAR WITH POPES, MERCHANT PRINCES AND THE PEOPLE. HIS BRIEF USEFUL LIFE WAS SPENT CREATING MAGNIFICENT WORKS IN PAINTING AND ARCHITECTURE THAT EARNED HIM IMMORTALITY.

RAPHAEL DIED ON HIS 37TH BIRTHDAY ON APRIL 6, 1520.

RAPHAEL OF URBINO

LEARNED FROM THE ANCIENTS AS WELL AS FROM THE ARTISTS OF HIS TIME. BY DIGGING UNDER THE STREETS OF ROME HE UNEARTHED IMPORTANT MONUMENTS AND SCULPTURES AND BECAME RENOWNED AS AN ARCHEOLOGIST.

UPON HIS APPOINTMENT AS SUPERINTENDENT OF ANTIQUITIES HE WROTE THAT HE HAD PREPARED HIMSELF BY: "HAVING BEEN VERY DILIGENT IN STUDYING THESE ANTIQUITIES, AND HAVING USED MUCH CARE IN FINDING AND MEASURING THEM CAREFULLY, AND BY READING CONTINUOUSLY GOOD AUTHORS..."

VASARI, IN HIS <u>LIVES</u> <u>OF</u> <u>THE</u> <u>ARTISTS</u> WROTE: "RAPHAEL, BESIDES BEING THE PERFECT ARTIST, WAS A PERFECT GENTLEMAN."

GOLZIO WROTE OF HIM:
RAPHAEL "...ALWAYS TAUGHT EVERYONE UNSELFISHLY AND HELPED THEM ALL."

RAPHAEL, SELF-PORTRAIT
ASHMOLEAN MUSEUM, OXFORD

"BINDO ALTOVITI", ART LOVER OF ROME, COMMISSIONED THE FAMOUS 30 YEAR OLD RAPHAEL TO PAINT HIS PORTRAIT.

RAPHAEL CREATED A SERIES OF CIRCLES WITHIN THE PORTRAIT TO KEEP OUR EYES CONSTANTLY MOVING. HE BEGINS THE INNER CIRCLE WITH ALTOVITI'S RIGHT EYE, THEN THE MOUTH AND NOSE. HE COMPLETES THIS OVAL WITH THE LEFT EYE.

THE NEXT MOVEMENT CARRIES US FROM THE HAT TO BROWN SUNLIT HAIR, CURVES AT THE NECK AND RETURNS UP THE SHADOWED HAIR TO THE HAT.

THE FINAL CIRCLE CALLS ATTENTION TO THE FRINGE OF THE GOLDEN BLOUSE AND THE RICH, ROYAL BLUE CLOAK. THE RELAXED HAND LEADS US BACK TO THE FACE.

STUDY FOR HEADS AND HANDS OF TWO APOSTLES   ASHMOLEAN MUSEUM, OXFORD

BINDO ALTOVITI   SAMUEL H. KRESS COLLECTION, NATIONAL GALLERY, WASHINGTON D.C.

RAPHAEL'S MURAL "SCHOOL OF ATHENS", CONTAINS MANY OF THE GREAT PHILOSOPHERS, MATHEMATICIANS AND SCHOLARS WHO LIVED DURING DIFFERENT AGES OF GREEK HISTORY.

PLATO POINTS UPWARD WITH HIS FINGER TO TELL US THAT THIS PHILOSOPHER WAS CONCERNED WITH IDEAS AND KNOWLEDGE AND NOT MATERIAL THINGS.

THE ARTIST USES PLATO TO DIRECT OUR ATTENTION TO HIS MAGNIFICENT PAINTINGS OF SCULPTURES, ARCHITECTURE AND THE DISTANT SKY WITH ITS WHITE CLOUDS.

ARISTOTLE, WITH OUT-STRETCHED ARM, HOLDS HIS HAND PALM DOWN AS THOUGH TO COVER THE EARTH. THIS BRILLIANT PHILOSOPHER TAUGHT ABOUT THE MATERIAL, MORAL AND ETHICAL PROBLEMS OF LIVING.

TWO STUDIES OF ANGELS   WICAR MUSEUM, LILLE

RAPHAEL HAS SHOWN HIS MASTERY OF

FORM

AND

COLOR

IN THIS INFORMAL GROUPING OF STUDENTS AND TEACHERS.

DETAIL: SCHOOL OF ATHENS

COMPLETE MURAL: SCHOOL OF ATHENS   THE VATICAN, ROME

RAPHAEL USED THE FACES OF HIS TEACHERS, FRIENDS AND FELLOW ARTISTS AS MODELS FOR THE FAMOUS CLASSICAL THINKERS AND STUDENTS IN HIS "SCHOOL OF ATHENS" MURAL PAINTED ON A WALL IN THE VATICAN CITY IN ROME.

RAPHAEL BROUGHT PLATO BACK TO LIFE IN THIS PAINTING BY GIVING HIM THE NOBLE FEATURES OF HIS FELLOW ARTIST LEONARDO DA VINCI.

WE CAN SEE RAPHAEL HIMSELF AND HIS ARTIST FRIEND SODOMA AS STUDENTS IN THIS IMAGINARY SCHOOL.

MICHELANGELO, ITALY'S GREATEST SCULPTOR AND PAINTER, SEEMS TO BE CARVED FROM COLORED STONE IN ANOTHER RAPHAEL PORTRAIT.

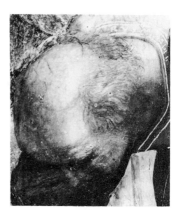

BRAMANTE, WHO WAS RAPHAEL'S TEACHER AND FRIEND, IS SHOWN AS EUCLID, THE FAMED GREEK MATHEMATICIAN.

LEFT DETAIL

RIGHT DETAIL

COMPLETE MURAL: SCHOOL OF ATHENS

THE VATICAN, ROME

"PORTRAIT OF A WOMAN", KNOWN AS "LA MUTA", IS A STUDY IN WHICH WE CAN SEE THE DIGNIFIED CHARACTER, RELAXED STRENGTH, CONCERN FOR PERSONAL APPEARANCE AND GOOD GROOMING OF THIS LADY.

RAPHAEL'S EYES REFLECT WITH THE FAITHFULNESS OF A MIRROR THE PAINTER-SCIENTIST'S OBJECTIVE SEARCH FOR TRUTH. AT THE SAME TIME HE SHOWS US THE CALMNESS AND BEAUTY OF HIS OWN INTERESTS AND THOUGHTS.

STUDY OF A HEAD AND HAND   BRITISH MUSEUM, LONDON

RAPHAEL'S DELIGHT IN THE ARCHITECTURE OF THE HUMAN BODY IS SEEN IN THE WAY HE HAS DESIGNED THIS PAINTING SO THAT THE FIGURE BECOMES A TEMPLE WITH THE LADY'S NECK AND HEAD RISING GRACEFULLY LIKE A BEAUTIFULLY COLUMNED DOME.

PORTRAIT OF A WOMAN   NATIONAL GALLERY, URBINO

"THE MARRIAGE OF THE VIRGIN" IS A MASTERPIECE THAT COMBINES PORTRAIT WITH LANDSCAPE AND ARCHITECTURAL PAINTING.

THE INTEREST IN THE FOREGROUND IS DIVIDED BY THE FIGURE OF THE RABBI WITH MARY AND HER FIVE BRIDESMAIDS ON THE LEFT AND JOSEPH AND HIS ATTENDANTS ON THE RIGHT. THE ARTIST USES HIS MASTERY OF PERSPECTIVE TO MOVE OUR EYES FROM THE MARRIAGE PARTY TO THE FIGURES GROUPED IN THE MIDDLE DISTANCE.

THEN HE DIRECTS US TO THE CENTRAL FLIGHT OF STEPS AND RAISES OUR EYES UP THE SYMMETRICAL COLUMNS TO THE GRACEFUL DOME SURROUNDED BY THE CLEAR BLUE SKY.

THERE ARE MANY COLORFUL DETAILS IN THIS MULTIPLE PAINTING FOR US TO SEE AND ENJOY.

STUDIES FOR FIGURE OF MINERVA AND OTHER STUDIES
ASHMOLEAN MUSEUM, OXFORD

THE MARRIAGE OF THE VIRGIN   BRERA, MILAN

THIS MOTHER AND CHILD KNOWN AS THE "TEMPI MADONNA" IS A WORK IN OIL PAINT THAT SHOWS US ONCE AGAIN RAPHAEL'S DEEP ADMIRATION AND RESPECT FOR ALL WOMEN.

NOTICE THE FIRM YET GENTLE POSITION OF THE MOTHER'S HANDS. THEY HOLD THE BABY SECURELY IN THE CRADLE OF HER ARMS. THE CHEEKS OF MOTHER AND CHILD PRESS TOGETHER LOVINGLY. RAPHAEL USES RICH COLORS TO GIVE ADDED MEANING TO HIS PAINTINGS.

AN ANGEL   ASHMOLEAN MUSEUM, OXFORD

THE SOFT PINK OF THE MADONNA'S DRESS, THE GOLDEN YELLOW OF HER SLEEVE, AND THE DELICATELY EMBROI- DERED SHAWL OF SOFT GREEN LEND WARMTH AND INTEREST TO THE CHARMING SCENE.

THE LIGHT **BROWN** EARTH, CALM WATER OF THE RIVER AND THE DISTANT LANDSCAPE RISE SOFTLY INTO THE TRANQUIL SKY.

TEMPI MADONNA   ALTE PINAKOTHEK, MUNICH

JUSTICE

THEOLOGY

POETRY

PHILOSOPHY

RAPHAEL WAS A MASTER OF MANY SUBJECTS — ARCHEOLOGY, POETRY, HISTORY AND PAINTING. HE ALSO ACHIEVED FAME AS AN ARCHITECT.

"THE DISPUTE OF THE SACRAMENTS" WAS THE FIRST OF THREE MURALS RAPHAEL PAINTED ON THE WALLS OF THE VATICAN ROOMS IN ROME. THESE MURALS WERE DEDICATED TO

TRUTH, GOODNESS, BEAUTY.

THIS MURAL WAS DESIGNED TO ILLUSTRATE TRUTH.

IN THIS ENLARGED DETAIL, WE CAN SEE THAT THE ARTIST USED THE FACES AND FIGURES OF TWO MEN WHO GREATLY INFLUENCED HIS ART AND LIFE.

DONATO BRAMANTE,

ARCHITECT OF ST. PETER'S CATHEDRAL, HOLDS A BOOK OF KNOWLEDGE WHICH HE IS SHOWING TO A HANDSOME YOUTH. THE YOUTH RESEMBLES

LEONARDO DA VINCI,

FOREMOST ARTIST, SCHOLAR AND SCIENTIST OF RAPHAEL'S TIME.

DETAIL: DISPUTE OF THE SACRAMENTS

COMPLETE MURAL: DISPUTE OF THE SACRAMENTS
THE VATICAN, ROME

RAPHAEL WAS CHOSEN BY BRAMANTE TO SUCCEED
HIM AS ARCHITECT OF ST. PETER'S. HE BECAME ONE
OF ITALY'S MOST LEARNED MEN, RESPECTED FOR HIS
KNOWLEDGE, ARCHITECTURE AND ART.

IN THIS DETAIL FROM "THE DISPUTE OF THE SACRAMENTS",
THE ARTIST SHOWS US THE METHOD BY WHICH SCAFFOLDING
WAS USED TO ERECT A BUILDING. WE SEE THE POSTS,
RAMPS AND CARPENTER'S PLATFORMS.

WE CAN STUDY THE WORKMEN MIXING CEMENT AND
THE HUT-LIKE MOUND OF STRAW USED TO BIND IT TO-
GETHER AND GIVE IT INTERNAL STRENGTH.

WE CAN OBSERVE HOW THE
ROAD ENTERS THE BUILDING
THROUGH THE ARCHED
OPENING, THE SLANTED
DESIGNS OF THE ROOFS,
THE SHAPES OF THE WINDOWS
AND THE PLACEMENT OF A
ROOF-TOP CHIMNEY.

RAPHAEL ALSO INCLUDES
THE BEAUTY OF NATURE
WITH ITS WAVES OF GREEN
GRASS, ITS UNCROWDED
TREES AND SPACIOUS SKY.

ARCHITECTURAL SKETCH   WICAR MUSEUM, LILLE

"PORTRAIT OF A WOMAN" IS A PERFECT EXAMPLE OF RAPHAEL'S SEARCH FOR HARMONY BETWEEN LINE AND LINE, FORM AND FORM, COLOR AND COLOR AND THE MAJESTIC, INSPIRING COMBINATION OF THE THREE.

HIS GENIUS IS SHOWN IN THE WAY HE MAKES THE FOLDS OF HER SLEEVE SURGE ACROSS THE FRONT OF THE WORK LIKE FOAMING WAVES IN A BREAKING SURF.

BEYOND THESE BILLOWS, WITH THEIR EDGES HEMMED IN SUNLIGHT, THE REPEATED WAVELETS OF HER WHITE BLOUSE FORM A GENTLE CURVE ALONG THE BEACH OF HER CHEST.

SKETCH OF A WOMAN

OUR ATTENTION IS CARRIED UP TO HER OVAL NECKLACE, THEN TO THE NECK AND TO HER DELICATELY FORMED HEAD AND FACE

THE LINES OF HER DRAPED VEIL CREATE A SHELL TO FRAME THIS BEAUTIFULLY PAINTED SYMPHONY.

SKETCH OF A WOMAN

PORTRAIT OF A WOMAN   PITTI, FLORENCE

IN "MADONNA AND CHILD WITH THE INFANT ST. JOHN" (CALLED "LA BELLE JARDINERE") RAPHAEL IS MORE THAN A PAINTER. HE IS A THOUGHTFUL STORY-TELLER. HE USES LINES, FORMS AND COLORS TO ADD MEANINGS TO HIS PAINTINGS BEYOND PLEAS- ING THE EYES.

STUDY FOR CHILD IN THE GARDEN   OXFORD
ASHMOLEAN MUSEUM

IN THIS MASTERPIECE, HE HAS COMBINED ALL THREE ELEMENTS AND GIVEN THEM REALITY BY CLEVERLY ALLOWING SPACE IN THE DESIGN.

THE MOTHER AND CHILDREN FORM A PYRAMID. SHE IS THE TOWER- ING PEAK WITH HER GRACEFUL HEAD AGAINST THE SKY. THE TWO LADS ARE THE PYRAMID'S CORNERSTONES, THE VERY MEAN- ING AND PURPOSE OF LIFE FOR HER.

NATURE SURROUNDS THE LOVING TRIO WITH A DELICATE BROWN AND GREEN BLANKET. IN THE DISTANCE, THE HILLS AND THE SPIRED CITY SEEM TO GUARD THEM. WHILE THE STANDING CHILD AND THE MADONNA STUDY EACH OTHER, THE KNEELING ST. JOHN REGARDS HIS COMPANION WITH ADMIRATION.

RAPHAEL HAS PAINTED AN INSPIRING STORY-PORTRAIT.

MADONNA AND CHILD WITH THE INFANT ST. JOHN (LA BELLE JARDINERE)   THE LOUVRE, PARIS

COMPLETE PAINTING : THE FOLIGNO MADONNA

IN THIS DETAIL TAKEN FROM THE CENTER OF "THE FOLIGNO MADONNA" RAPHAEL CONSTRUCTS WITH HIS CREATIVE MIND AND MAGNIFICENTLY TRAINED EYES A CITY OF TEMPLES AND MONUMENTS IN THE ANCIENT LAND OF ISRAEL.

HIGH-RANGING MOUNTAINS MIRRORING THE BLUE SKY ARE ENCIRCLED BY A GOLDEN ARC OF SUNLIGHT WHICH EMBRACES UNDER ITS PROTECTIVE DOME, BUILDINGS, LANDSCAPE, PEOPLE, ANIMALS AND, IN FACT, EVERYTHING WITH ITS WARMING GLOW.

RAPHAEL STUDIED THE WORKS OF THE GREATEST PHILOSOPHERS. HE KNEW THAT NATURE, AS WELL AS MANKIND, WAS AN IMMENSE AND IMPORTANT TEACHER OF KNOWLEDGE.

RAPHAEL USED HIS EYES TO SEE WITH SCIENTIFIC CLARITY. HE WORKED CONSTANTLY TO TRAIN THE HAND THAT HELD HIS BRUSHES AND PENS TO

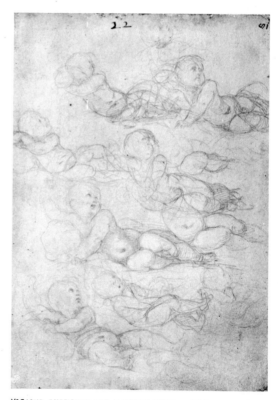

VARIOUS SKETCHES FOR A CHRIST CHILD   BRITISH MUSEUM, LONDON

PUT DOWN ON HIS WOODEN PANELS, PAPERS, CANVASES AND WALLS ALL THE RICH BEAUTY HIS EYES HAD BEHELD.

THE MADONNA OF FOLIGNO   THE VATICAN, ROME

"VISION OF A KNIGHT" TELLS A TIMELESS STORY. RAPHAEL'S SLEEPING SOLDIER DREAMS OF WAR AND PEACE. HIS HEAD LIES IN THE TERRITORY OF LAW AND ORDER. HIS HEART RESTS IN THAT OF PEACE AND LOVE. HIS STRONG RIGHT ARM SUPPORTS HIS BODY ON HIS SHIELD WHILE HIS OTHER ARM RESTS AT HIS SIDE.

THE MAID OF LAW AND ORDER CARRIES A SWORD AND A BOOK OF LAWS. HER COSTUME IS FITTED FOR ACTION. HER HAIR IS GROOMED AND BOUND TO THE BACK OF HER HEAD.

THE MAID OF PEACE AND LOVE CARRIES A BRANCH OF FLOWERS AND FINGERS HER STRAND OF BEADS. HER LOOSE HAIR AND GATHERED DRESS ADD SOFTNESS AND BEAUTY TO HER FACE AND FIGURE.

THE YOUNG SOLDIER AND THE SAPLING TREE ARE SIGNPOSTS ALONG THE ROAD OF LIFE. ON ONE PATH IS A WALLED FORTRESS CITY, THE OTHER LEADS TO QUIET WATERS.

DREAM OF A KNIGHT   NATIONAL GALLERY, LONDON

VISION OF A KNIGHT   NATIONAL GALLERY, LONDON

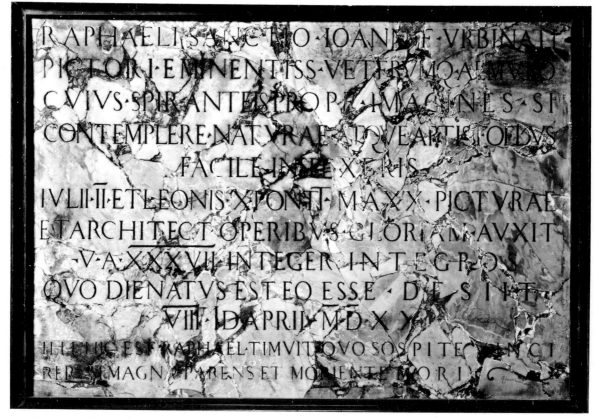

THE STONE ON RAPHAEL'S TOMB IN THE PANTHEON, ROME